► IN THE STONEWORKS

► **IN THE**

John Ciardi

Rutgers University Pre

STONEWORKS

New Brunswick, New Jersey ◀

Library of Congress Catalogue Card Number: 61–10256

ISBN: 0–8135–0375–2

*Acknowledgment is made to the following magazines
in which some of these poems were first published:*
The Antioch Review, The Atlantic, Chicago Choice,
Coastlines, Harper's Magazine, Impetus, Ladies' Home Journal,
The New Yorker, The Poet (*Scotland*), Poetry, Poetry
Dial, Prairie Schooner, Quarterly Review of Literature,
Saturday Review, Think, The Tuftonian, The Urbanite.

Manufactured in the United States of America

Third Printing, 1971

To Milton and Cele Hebald, stoneworkers

CONTENTS

Part III ▶ Natures

I ▸ BACK HOME IN POMPEII

The sea shines. Wind-raked, the waters run light
strand by strand. Wind-plowed, they fold
light into the furrows. Wind-winnowed, they toss
spume ends; and rainbows and the ghosts
of rainbows leap, drift fading across an
enormous look, like breath at the poles.
All burning in motion. All sanctioned and told.
All sent of the creature's warmth in the world's cold.

The sea shines. Tremulous over its crushing hunch
to the world's end, it shakes the entire
tree of light to the sky-top, and the gulls
blow off like leaves that seem never to land
but to catch fire in air and be wholly consumed—
all back to fire and air before
they can take weight and fall. A day,
another day, burns upward in the great eye, and away.

It takes a god to say "the sea shines" each first time
into the day, as his eye goes, thought by thought
before him, calling forth from lead-deeps and blazings,
from far-silver and shore-mica, imagination
by imagination, the dazzle
of what will be sung and sung, age by age,
man by man, of the god in him, as each
stands churned in his lit veins on his lit beach.

The man stands in god's place on that shore,
opening the eye there is—
man's, god's, or beast's—for seeing the world lit
in the wind from origin. "The sea shines,"
he says, and a god could say no more,
having once begun entirely to imagine
by what world he stands, in the pour
of what abundance, on what hammered shore.

4 ► The Dolls

Night after night forever the dolls lay stiff
by the children's dreams. On the goose-feathers of the rich,
on the straw of the poor, on the gypsy ground—
wherever the children slept, dolls have been found
in the subsoil of the small loves stirred again
by the Finders After Everything. Down lay
the children by their hanks and twists. Night after night
grew over imagination. The fuzzies shed, the bright
buttons fell out of the heads, arms ripped, and down
through goose-feathers, straw, and the gypsy ground
the dolls sank, and some—the fuzziest and most loved—
changed back to string and dust, and the dust moved
dream-puffs round the Finders' boots as they dug,
sieved, brushed, and came on a little clay dog,
and a little stone man, and a little bone girl, that had kept
their eyes wide open forever, while all the children slept.

Back home in Pompeii
birds crunched underfoot,
stones flew away,
statues began to bow.

Government wrote
our clauses and conditions,
then as now.
But, egged in stone,
a saved worm curled alone
to hatch through the inscriptions.

Some thought to run and were
the first down.
The weather laid a ton
on every breath.
I brought you water there
and watched it hiss away.
"It's an elaborate death,"
I heard you say.
And then the rafters broke.

Storms later, we awoke
and strolled among ourselves
in the excavated bed—
stone castings on stone shelves.

How had we fled,
leaving so neat a foot
cast in the mountain's soot?
these hands in a glass case?
and, like an artifact,
the fragment of a face?

One of us lay intact
for anyone to see
the stone-stored human form
curled like the stone-saved worm
in a last agony.

Well, that's that.
Settled down
and starting to get fat
in another town
oceans away,
we only come to see
a curiosity
on holiday.

All in a dream of the time it was
(Kissing the corpse on its bombproof nose)
I winked at a peach that gave me a buzz,
But when I rubbed her she had no fuzz.
A sad chair stared, heaped with our clothes.

All in the light of the moon that came
(The bottles empty, the switches thrown)
I lost my wallet, I changed my name,
I saw the colonel go down aflame.
There stood the chair, our only one.

All in a heap on the chair that stood
(Polaris neither rising nor setting)
I told no evil, I saw no good
Except those sad few sticks of wood,
Like a ghost I had been forgetting.

All in a row in the law that wrought
(Some still listed and some still lost)
I sighted squinty, my tracers caught,
The sad chair blew up like a thought.
She snored her whiskey. I turned and tossed.

All in a dream of the thought that blows
The moon in the window, the ghost on the chair,
The one sad chair heaped with our clothes,
I kissed her corpse on its bombproof nose,
And left her dead and went out for air.

All in a dream of the time it is
(The colonels coming, the colonels going)
Since Tokyo sizzled her star-spangled sizz,
I got a medal for writing this,
And an oak-leaf cluster because it was snowing.

All in the hush of the snow that fell
(Tojo dancing for everyone's crime)
We swung the hammer, we rang the bell,
But the only reason it wasn't Hell
We went to was—we won, that time.

All in a haggle of what we won
(The corncob rampant above the noose)
The sad chair stood, our only one
I wish, now all is said and done,
We had shared that sadness, but what's the use?

Ah could we wake in mercy's name—
the church mouse in each other's eyes
forgiven, the wart hog washed in flame
confessed—when paunch from paunch we rise,
false and unmartyred, to pretend
we dress for Heaven in the end.

To look and not to look away
from what we see, but, kindly known,
admit our scraping small decay
and the gross jowls of flesh on bone—
think what a sweetness tears might be
in mercy, each by each set free.

Only Success is beast enough
to stop our hearts. Oh twist his tail
and let him howl. When best we love
we have no reason but to fail,
in reason learning as we live
we cannot fail what we forgive.

That mouse is in your eyes and mine.
That wart hog wallows in our blood.
But, ah, let mercy be our sign,
and all our queer beasts, understood,
shall rise, grown admirable, and be,
in mercy, each by each set free.

I

In the garden of the hurricane's eye, a bird
wound tight to sun shook on a bough, shook out
blood-music from the heart-pump of the light;
and all the day's wood woke, trembling with song.
From vines like conflagrations of the air,
from weightless tops of green, from bearing boughs
nodding their fruits, and over meadows glazed
like birthday cakes candled with flickering flowers,
the morning wind of bird song swelled its way
into the waking thought of man and woman
wound in their mosses at the edge of time.

He lay carved dark and naked, one root-arm
outflung across the moss, half-deep in moss.
She, on her side, lay folded in the sleep
between his arm and body, her breasts borne
against the brown withes of his ribs, her hair
spilled on his shoulder, one arm and one knee
locking her birth to his. Like vine on tree
she knit upon him. Like the sun-wound birds
her heart began. And like the morning song
that fluttered the flower-candles in the sun,
and stirred the leaping blazes of the vines,

she stirred in him and woke. A rainbow bent
to her first-opened eyes. Like light and shade
a smile played on her lips. She raised herself
slowly on one moss-printed elbow, leaning
between him and the light, and knew at once,
as she stared down at him, how he would wake.
She tested tremblingly with her slow eyes
the knottings of his body. He looked foolish
lying so far from knowledge, his mouth open.
His useless nipples, like two hairy shells,
slid sidewise on his sleep. She almost laughed—

to be so knit with powers and vestiges
and still to sleep, while every sun-wound bird
shook the day's wood with song, and his own blood
ran like new singing rivers from his heart-hump
to the bronze blood-webbed gourd burled in his thighs.
This time she laughed aloud. It was that laugh
more than all bird song brought his eyes to rest
from their lost wander in themselves. His lids
blew back like mist. At the sky-top he saw
the storm's clear eye look down, then look away.
He heard a wind move and the sea change sound.

She laughed again, but only in herself,
and touched him with a finger on one nipple.
His flung arm grew around her. Silently
she swelled upon it as upon the wood
of which she was the leaf, the fruit, and pod.
The laughter in her bloomed into a fire:
she was the vine blazed up the bird-swept trees,
he was the trunk and forest of all sleep
and waking, and one weather raged them both.
She clung against its rip, then fell away
backward from trunk to moss. The tree fell with her.

Out of its ripped roots rose the blood-webbed snake.

II
The birds had shut themselves. From broken boughs
the vines lashed like loose lines, their pennants torn.
The meadow-candles, doused, blew down and lay
like strings in mud. The man and woman lay
lashed to themselves, nearer than Paradise,
a weather in them Heaven wept to bear.
All she had wakened knowing, he would learn.

All he had wakened answering, she would be.
The weather killed and rested. Beetles baked
like gravel in the mud. The sucking sun
glued them to clay again. The eighth day burned.

All round them now inquiring angels passed,
and found no one tree, but the fruit of all
baked into clay with beetles, heads of birds,
and the torn vines of that dismasted sleep.
The woman looked up from between two rocks
and thought "Is this the end? Is there an end?"
The man said nothing but refused their alms,
salvaged what could be of spoiled fruit, dug roots
and brought them to her. "Is it time to go?"
she asked beside him, watching the light angels
strolling and taking note. He did not answer.

All night he lay beside her, silent. Silent
he woke and dug a cave back from their rocks.
Silent, he combed the wood among the angels.
And silent at the shore where they had moored
he scraped for mussels, slipped, gashed his arm open,
and left his first blood on the water. (Later,
an angel noted that the ship's reflection,
lying across the cove's glaze, must have touched
the bloodstain in its instant on the water,
for when they put to sea one jib was red.
And all the weathers of Heaven could not bleach it.)

That night he lay again without a word
half in the unfinished cave, his scarred arm left
like a new bone in moonlight, while his head
lay in the shadow he had dug. She, waking,
sat by him weeping softly for his blood,

then bent and kissed the scar—tenderly first;
then with a sobbing passion pressed her lips
into his flesh, so hard the scar broke blood.
He woke in pain, and it was then he spoke.
"Eve," he said from his dark, and his red arm
locked round her till she moaned for her crushed breath.

The one-eyed moon lay on them openly
when they fell spent, apart. She knew his name
and said it to herself where she lay from him,
face up into the moon. "Adam," she said,
as if a night bird knocked inside her heart;
and waited for that knock, knew it would come
one night as they lay locked. "Adam," she said,
and like a moonglow edged back to his side.
"How dark he is," she thought, "even the moon
leaves him half shadowy." But when she lay
beside him, she, too, darkened and went out.

Then a branch moved, and both of them lay lit.

III
Before dawn he was waiting at the shore.
The sun rose through the rigging of the ship.
He heard their voices drifting on the water
and did not know what language they were speaking
but heard shouts of command, hurrying sounds
such as he had not heard them make before,
and knew that they were leaving. As he knew
that one, the tallest and the whitest Captain
of all that crew of Captains, would come to him
there on the shore before the ship hove round
into the weather and was gone. The ship

broke out a white jib, then a red. He smiled—
a sword-smile drawn on at the edge of battle—
his blood would sail there far as the sea wound
into God's eye. The weather God denied
would hoist one flag in Heaven, if no other.
He saw Him then: an eye in his mind's eye,
a calm raged round by storms. And at the center?
Was that it? to be locked in calm, but powerless
to calm what raged? To pity God the lusts
that hurled Him round, yet kept their distance from Him?
He bowed his head to knowledge. The Angel came.

White as a noon cloud swelling on the sea,
yet shot through by a flame of ice, the Angel
stood off the earth and breezes circled him
like sunset doves, their wings both red and white,
and neither, and all three in the same instant.
"The orders were to drive you from the Garden."
And he: "It was His eye moved and let in
the rage around it. Now, what garden is there
but what I make myself?" The Angel nodded,
and from his hawk-head one white feather fell.
The man watched it descend through all one age.

"You still may choose," God's bird said. "Come or stay.
This age is ended and the ship turns back."
Crouched at the fern-edge of the wood, the woman
shivered at the man's laugh. She watched him turn
full circle east to west and saw him roll
the world into his eye. She felt his look,
felt it approach; thought once their eyes had met,
but his passed on, and she crouched back afraid.
As if out of her fear, the whole wood started
its waterfall of bird song; leaf and fruit
came on at once; the meadows lit their candles.

"Has He a garden not ringed round by rages?"
he said. And the Angel, suddenly man-faced:
"You stay then?" But the man felt his first power.
"I won't have words put into my mouth, not even
by a half-God in kindness. My words are not
'I stay' but 'You go.' " Sadly, the Hawk smiled:
"Take this, then," and he put a burning branch
into the man's hand. Then the ship was gone.
The man turned, flag in hand, and saw her risen

out of the ferns. And waved. And the brand burned.

There was a tree whose leaves were flowers.
Rainbow deck by deck it tiered
Into original light—a weird
And central system blazed with towers.

The black trunk gnarled and sent away
Whole horizontal nebulae,
While the main shaft, split into three,
Struck through the dome of night and day.

It was my tree. Its leaves my flowers.
I woke under it all one lawn.
Like small monks who had died and gone
To Heaven, bees intoned great hours.

Like small humped monks with lighted souls
They prayed their spirals to its blooms.
And radiant as the promised tombs
Of martyrs, rose in aureoles.

It was my tree of dappled swings.
I floated under it all one weather.
The bees and I turned gold together.
Time stroked us with first wings.

Till wind by wind, in storms of shreds,
The flowers spun off, the buds stood bare.
One winter I was passing there
And saw its fruit—like shrunken heads.

> *And if you do not weep,*
> *at what are you used to weeping?*
> —UGOLINO

The little one
chilled paler and paler
till the smile in her
wisped off
like breath in a frost.

Then, last, her eyes went out.
By that nightfall
the snow on the sill
had let out glass claws,
and what man was not scratched
could have no tears in this world
nor hope of dear smiling.

All our silences walked those rooms,
walked us,
tore and took
what we did not say.

"This is what Nothing is,"
said our silences.
"And this," said the winter mounds
that had to be blasted open
even for so little a one
to slide into
                to Nothing.

"Good-morning," says the Fine Brisk Man in the mirror,
"And what shall you do today?"
"I shall part my hair, I suspect, as I always do.
Or maybe another way."

"That wouldn't work long," says the Excellent Man in the mirror.
"A man's hair leans like all the things of his life
into habituation. It would only tousle
once it has dried. That would displease your wife."

"The hair of her pleasure," I grin at the man in the mirror,
"does not grow on my head, though I part it with care."
"*Today*, I said," says the man. "Save that for night."
"The time to shoot is when the quail's in air."

"Not very clever," says the Good Sound Man in the mirror.
"Have you no serious thought, no thought
appropriate to my better sense of composure?"
"No, sir, I have not."

"Well, what of China and Lebanon and Algeria?
What of the bickering flags on the winds today?
How can you see life steadily and see it whole
in that irresponsible way?"

"Sir," I say to the Clean-Shaven Man in the mirror,
"I recall you when your face was stuck with sleep,
and your chin draggled with whiskers.
You were not, I think, quite so deep

poised and sententious then. Can soap and water,
lather, a razor, and a dash of smell
have wrought all this in something like five minutes?
Try it on someone who doesn't know you so well,

or I swear I'll tousle you till you never slicken,
gum up your eyes, and dangle hemp from your chin.
You shined accessory to an attaché case,
you're not taking me in.

Aren't you the brat who used to steal from Woolworth's?
And your own mother's purse to get to the show?
Haven't I seen you puking drunk?" Says the Proper
Prosperous Middle-aged Man in the mirror, "Really now!"

"And who cried like a ninny when that girl chucked him—
what was her name? And though he took the jam
and wore the medals, almost froze on the triggers
when the Zeroes tried to ram?

And who do you think was saving the world's sobriety
the night you bit the garter-belt from Nell?"
"— Well," says the Very Suave Man in the mirror, "so it goes.
But we mustn't—now must we?—tell."

Nobody told me anything much. I was born
free to my own confusions, though in hock
to Mother and Father Sweatshop's original stock
in Boston, Mass., four families to a john.
The spire of the Old North Church, like a tin horn
upside down on the roofs, was our kitchen clock,
and dropped the hours like rock onto a rock
over the Hull Street graveyard. "Gone. All gone,"

it thunked above the dead. The smells were sad.
And there were rats, of course, but nailed tin
could keep them down (or at least in)
to a noise between the hours. The graveyard had
left us a son in real estate and the lad
had grown to father our landlord, though Frank Glynn
was the wart-on-the-nose that came with a sneaky grin
to collect the rent. Till he died to Hell. Too bad.

Nobody told me anything much, and that
so wrong it cost me nothing—not even love—
to lose it. All but the Boss, the Cop and the Ghost of
the Irish Trinity. Those I sweated at
so hard I came up hating. But still grew fat
in a happy reek of garlic, bay, and clove.
I was crazy, of course, but always at one remove.
I tried on faces as if I were buying a hat.

Home was our Asylum. My father died
but my mother kept talking to him. My sisters screamed.
My aunt muttered. My uncle got drunk and dreamed
three numbers a night for a quarter with cock-eyed
Charlie Pipe-Dreams who moseyed along half-fried
every morning at seven. The old boy schemed
for twenty years that I knew of before he was reamed
by Family Morticians. But I'll say this—he tried.

Nobody told me anything much. Nobody had
anything much to tell me. I rolled my own
and scrounged for matches. How could I have known
everything about us was full-moon mad?
Or that I'd find few saner? It wasn't bad.
Someone always answered the telephone
when it had rung too long. You got only a tone
when they finally called you—far away and sad.
But it didn't matter. There would have been nothing to say.
Later they changed the number and we moved away.

"Time," said the spectacled skeletal lady
back of the desk, "is this library card.
You may sign for some but not for all.
Return what you've borrowed when due."

"Thank you," I said with the pleasure of loathing,
"I'll browse a bit, but a book not worth owning
is not worth reading. I'll borrow nothing
I set my own eyes to, and give nothing back."

"Sir," said the spectacled skeletal lady
back of the desk, "in this allegory
you read from my shelves or not at all.
Go look for yourself: there *are* no bookstores."

I looked all right: the town was a desert:
even the signs on the stores were blanked out.
"I've got to read something," I yelled at the sun.
Said a gentle cop, "The library's that way."

Back I went, damn her. "What have you done?"
"I?" said the spectacled skeletal lady
back of the desk. "I've done nothing whatever
but tell you the truth, when you dare believe it.

Will you sign for your card, please? Others are waiting.
The rules are just what I said and no more:
you may sign for some but not for all,
and return what you've borrowed when due."

"Keep it!" I shouted and heard through my anger
all of the reading room hissing for silence.
Insolent geese! I swear Hell's a barnyard.
"I'll write my own book!" I shouted still louder.

"For that," said the spectacled skeletal lady
back of the desk, "you apply at the office."
"Ah," said the gentle cop, climbing the stairs,
"you found it I see. But you'll have to be quiet."

Aunt Mary died of eating twelve red peppers
 after a hard day's work. The doctor said
 it was her high blood pressure finished her.
 As if disease were anything to Aunt Mary
 who had all of her habits to die of! But imagine
 a last supper of twelve red peppers, twelve
 of those crab-apple size dry scorchers
 you buy on a string at Italian groceries,
 twelve of them fried in oil and gobbled off
 (Aunt Mary was a messy eater)—and then,
 to feel the room go dizzy, and through your blood
 the awful coming on of nothing more
 than twelve red peppers you know you shouldn't have eaten
 but couldn't help yourself, they were so good.

Now what shall I pray for gluttonous Aunt Mary
 who loved us till we screamed? Even poor Mother
 had more of Aunt Mary's love than she could live with,
 but had to live with it. I am talking now
 of a house with people in it, every room
 a life of a sort, a clutter of its own.
 I am talking of a scene in the palm of God
 in which one actor dies of twelve red peppers,
 one has too many children, one a boy friend,
 two are out of work, and one is yowling
 for one (offstage) to open the bathroom door.
 This is not the scene from the palm of God
 in which the actors hold God in their palms,
 nor the scene in which the actors know their prayers—

it is the scene in which Aunt Mary died
 and nobody knew anything, least of all
 Aunt Mary. In her red-hot transformation
 from gluttony into embalmer's calm

and candlelight, I cried a hypocrite tear.
But it was there, when I had seen Aunt Mary
bloodlet for God, that I began to see
what scene we are. At once I wept Aunt Mary
with a real tear, forgiving all her love,
and its stupidities, in the palm of God.
Or on a ledge of time. Or in the eye
of the blasting sun. Or tightroped on a theorem.
—Let every man select his own persuasion:
I pray the tear she taught me of us all.

Said the Damaged Angel to the Improved Ape:
"Time is a hard road. I've come from others,
and longer, but never
so choking a dust, nor stones
so honed to the instep. This way's a crippler."

Answered the Ape, fingering the strings
of a first thought: "Measure's
whatever you're used to. I've
traveled no easier, ever, and, yes,
it's a crippler at last, but it does for what's doing."

"A thought!" said the Angel astonished. "And worthy
of me, though I say so. I'm learning there's more
to you, surely,
than met my eye first
when I stopped in the shade to lament like a creature."

"Your arrogance," answered the Ape, still improving,
and scratching a memory dark in the Tree he was leaving,
"reminds me of something
near as a mother tongue saying
we've more here in common than shade and the need of it."

"Enough," said the Damaged Angel, his legal training
still evident. "Our natures teach our natures
no trespass on common ground.
We've nowhere, it's certain, to go
but each other, and shall we begin, since we must?"

"There arises at once," said the Ape, now improving
faster and faster with practice, "the question of sex.
The 'begats,' you recall
take particular doing. Myself,
I am partial to being the male of whatever we sign to."

"No, no," said the Angel, "though damaged, I'm still
the more heavenly part of what follows, and clearly
the aspirant, therefore
the male, of whatever
told species may flow from the womb of commandment."

"If mind is your weapon," the Ape, now concerned
not to improve too fast, replied, "I must tell you
you haven't convinced me.
Which leaves it, I'll argue, my turn
to suggest. Let's fight for it: power's a sure master."

So they fought and begat and the book of their doing
is long in the telling, with most left uncertain,
and endless the names
of their children, and not one
among them soul-sure of his father and mother.

It took four flowerboats to convoy my father's black
Cadillac cruiser out to St. Mike's and down
deeper than all salt. It was a very successful
funeral my mother remembers remembering. *Imagine*
what flowers! Even the undertaker was surprised,
he told me! He came with only two flowercars.
He had to send his son all over town like crazy
to find two more, there were so many. Imagine!

And when the funeral went to circle the block three
times—those days they did that: it was like the man
coming home again three times for his soul to remember—
we started, and when the first cars came around, the last
ones were still blocking the street! Even
the undertaker was surprised! He had to go around two
blocks instead of one to make the circles for the soul!
You were too small to remember, but imagine!

. . . It was my first cruise: the streets ahead a groundswell
of flowers, the wind ripping petals like spume from a wave,
the hearse bobbing nattily in the troughs, powerful
and in ballast, dead into the flower-stripping wind, and steady.
Man! what a big day at sea it was in that wind past all
the shores that stood-to and moved with us through
the ports of the black cabin my mother made of her flesh
in the black Cadillac cruiser I midshipped in. I mean, God,

it was a regatta, I tell you, she told me,
half of which I remember, and half of which
I remember being told after I had forgotten it once.
There were thirty-three powerboats from the Figli d'Italia
alone; seventeen (sometimes nineteen, and, once, twenty-seven)
from Metropolitan; and half the North End in the rest. That's

ninety, or over a hundred, and, some days, more, not
counting the flowerboats and the hearse.
                                        I had to go
(well, so I did, but I mean years later) to Venice and lean over
a cortege of gondolas stroked under the Ponte di Rialto
and out the big circle to the Campo Santo, like a trooping
of black swans on a fire-glaze, before I remembered clean
what an armada my father died into, sailing his flower-storm out
on the wind of the longest going my mother ever
sailed to sea or success on; and still breathes the forty-year-
old salt of new, between black and triumph.

Seabirds on their carrousel
danced the spinning wind offshore
one of the days the world went well.

The battleship Potemkin wore
a flag of weather at its top.
It passed those birds and passed no more.

The Big Mo had no time to stop.
It pushed the weather to the East,
and there its shells began to drop.

The wolfpack's Commodore at least
had his own skin to think about,
and once torpedoes were released

he dove, and could not have looked out
to see the seabirds' holiday.
Given the facts, there's room to doubt

he would have noticed anyway.
And when the depth charge made a mess
of all the tricks in which he lay,

the seabirds, full of their success
at being easy on the blow,
beyond perfection or distress,

never saw the navies go.

Saint X in winter: the stone angels change
into white overcoats above the dead.
The stone rhymes end in drifts, yet speak the same.
The same, whatever is or is not said:
   "I was a traveler, too, and I have come
   to winter stones, immovable and numb.
      Stranger, rub clean this name!"

Whatever is or is not to be known,
the dead compare to nothing. It is easy
to pass that prayer awash on every stone.
Tick-tick, an elm counts in the frost. And He
   who winds the main of ice in Labrador
   may build brick churches for a metaphor,
      but who knows that for sure?

I pose here as the man turned out of time,
asking whatever is or is not meant
to stand into some sequence for the mind.
Nonsense, of course: I came, I was not sent:
   the air grew thick inside and I walked out
   to lean against the weather with no thought
      but to smell out the North.

So am I on my own, a happened chance
caught on its five wits among bundled angels
whose noses run icicles and whose hands
hold out hydrangeas—pieces of a day
   touching themselves to sight, but lacking mind
   to ask the dead of winter by what wind
      or whose, worlds are blown blind.

Whatever is or is not to be seen
a man could live to if he had a cause.

Tick-tick, the elms speak theirs, the angels weep
blue crystals, and the stonecut rhymes at Law
   tighten inside the natural press that locks
   Saint X together in his building blocks
     until the day he cracks.

Whatever is or is not to be guessed,
and for no reason any man can give,
all stones fall over. I forget the rest.
My guess is, winter is a self-wound thing.
   If Saint X in his cracking stones sees more,
   maybe all seasons are a metaphor,
     but who knows that for sure?

A twilight of opal hazes
muffles the day shut,
brushing with clear glazes
the lawn, the cube-cut
privet, the licorice street,
the metal-colored fleet
in the parking lot,
each box a ceramic yacht.

From far as Brueghel's mind
landscapes of drowned trees
and sunken fields unwind.
I sit and look at these—
empty as they are—through
a window, and think of you,
as once in the lost wars
I fell asleep to stars.

I wish that you might be
here, at the-sill-there-is,
to watch how seamlessly
light touches the abyss,
and how across the way
from where the world turns gray,
a boy the size of a match
is playing a golden catch.

Everywhere I turn
the world is sitting through
the stillness of an urn.
If ever a wind blew,
no leaf now in the world
foresees it will be hurled,
recalls it ever stirred,
brushed by breeze or bird.

Now the boy moves and now
nothing moves at all,
except my look, a slow
turning-in, like the fall
of light itself, like thought.
I think how you are not
here. Yet if time is true
all that I see is you.

From left to right of haze,
to the last light shed
on the parked cars' glaze
in the still gleaming dead
black of the empty street,
in silence thick as heat,
you are the scene there is
between day and abyss.

Take this drowned twilight as
a gift that I may send.
And as you watch it pass,
seamless, so may it mend
every divided thought
whether to be or not,
turning into such night
as drowns again in light.

It is Spring, darling, and the five feathers
a-tickle in my wits, those five furry antennae
the spun self spins out to the rayed weathers,
twitch and receive new airs. A slight uncanny
ripple stirs the skin. I learn how far
into the threaded wood the young wolf reaches,
his sense trembling, turning hair by hair
the prescience wound in creatures.

It is Spring, and never again perfectly, but always
again as if the language born of things
spoke itself whole, I take days
as if spoken, light as it brings
great green scripts into view. And since my most
green-spoken and green-written tongue is you,
I speak and read my senses, season-tossed,
to their first rushing Logos ringing through

the morning of the world begun,
the first arriving airs
through which the young wolves run
along the quick, cocked to their dowsing ears
and instant noses. Darling, I am slow
and human and the wood outruns my blood.
I fill with tongues I do not wholly know,
with prowling senses never understood,

tracking my five wits to their deepest den,
where you wait in the first of time again.

In the stoneworks under God, the broken statuary
formed ranks like an army in storage. Spiders wove
halos for the headless. Detailed worms
lay rusted shut in the ringbolts, link by link.

Upstairs, in the tree-light, shapes blurred. Briar
had taken the stone stumps, grass the floor plan.
Three first trunks still shored a pediment,
and there Gods, weathered featureless, enacted

half-gestures over the gravels of themselves.
But swallows had fouled the inscriptions,
and out of hanging muds the fledglings flamed,
ravenous and shrill. The air creaked with their hunger.

In the sky, an ice-age coiled, and let fall light.
What could be light. What was light-as-it-is,
passing the time it takes till even the stoneworks
under the stoneworks stand bare to the unmade day.

Here, time concurring (and it does),
Lies Ciardi. If no kingdom come,
A kingdom was. Such as it was,
This one, beside it, is a slum.

II ► VOICES

. . . By wanting to and being able; hand and eye
married, and the line born of one motion
between them, a proportion in love.

Mystery? What child is born explained?
Yet all our alleys babble under their laundry
that the means of life are known.
                                        This head now—
I took it from the shoulders of a child,
anatomized it, held it in my eye,
then joined my hand and eye. And there it is:

not what it was, but what I made of it,
hand and eye at the work they understand.
You know how or you don't. But to know how

is first to be born of a people, to be
the bearer of their seed—son, husband, father
of the thing married and born of the marriage.

God's gift? That, too, is known, or isn't. My people
knew birth and death forever, *then* learned God.
Truth after truth: men have their work to do,

and know how or they don't, and then lie down
to rise or not, but dark in the same death
that leaves the flies their proofs and the saints theirs.

I am no mystifier of such matters.
It is the nose on your face I see, and your face
formed from itself, its mathematics

of tangible wonder the thing I know how to do,
want to, and am able. To find my mind's eye in the world,
and give my hand in marriage.

*(Spoken as he waits to make his
entrance for the final scene)*

My father died, my mother married.
I can say, in general, I disapproved
Of the lengths to which things had been carried
Even before Ophelia was removed.

There's the king-my-father, and my own sweet chick,
And her father to boot, and my good old drinking
Stinking school pals. I could feel sick
If I thought about it, and I *am* thinking.

Two were the best, and two were measly,
And one a fool, and that makes five.
God, I could swallow my bodkin easily.
Mother, what are we doing alive?

Let spooks, I say, do their own killing.
Do you hear, Horatio? Well, all's not lost:
My uncle's breathing, but God willing,
The fashion in kings is to turn ghost.

It's the rage in Denmark all this season:
The best, the measly, the in-between,
And the worst—right down to the worm of treason—
Are spooking out on my lady the Queen.

Mother, Mother, bring me a cup.
My throat is cut as any pig's.
I'll bleed until I fill it up,
And you must drink while my uncle jigs.

Denmark's dead and the world is dying.
Horatio, run away and live.
A man could get to the moon with trying,
Or cross the sea in a sieve.

There are spooks in the cellarage. Mothers in the hay.
Worms in the crown. And school's recessed.
My girl and her daddy are stinking up the clay.
And I'm very carelessly dressed,

Like my girl and her daddy and my daddy too.
It's hard, Horatio, being quality folks.
I could be as simple and as loyal as you
If the egg of our making had a choice of yolks.

I'd choose the smallest yolk of all:
No royalty, no loyalty, but all sincerity.
I'd be no prince and I'd live in no hall.
I'd be born an actor and just play at being me.

Then every time I cried, and every time I died,
I'd listen for applause, and I'd damn them all
If they coughed, or whispered, or sat dry-eyed,
Or didn't have me up for a curtain call.

I'd be me, do you see, but all the me I'd be
Would be seven turns a week, with the Wednesday matinee.
And both kings, in street clothes, would drink with me.
And I'd have a turn at bouncing in the hay

With the chick that plays Ophelia, and now and then
With the wench that plays the queen to bust a gusset.
And the passions we'd tatter, m'lords and gentlemen,
Would be art, were you competent to discuss it.

Ready, Horatio? Let's get that duel done with.
Is it art or life that piles the corpses high?
You've had luck enough: you've had a prince to run with.
Come in now and watch me try to die.

My father and my chick and her father are dead.
Rosencrantz and Guildenstern are done for.
And the wench that plays my mother's fast to bed,
But not to the bed she got a son for.

Born and done for, dead and married.
I must say again, in general, that I disapprove
Of the lengths to which I feel things have been carried.
And there's still a cord of corpses to remove.

To it, Horatio. It's time again to go.
But is it art or life comes next? And I—
I've rehearsed it all so often I don't know—
Am I Hamlet, or *a* Hamlet? When I die

Will it be in blood, Horatio, or merely in the script?
All a-thump or in a nicely practiced fall?
My shirt is slit already. Will my soul get ripped?
And shall I rise to judgment or a curtain call?

Once, from a cliff, my countryman Marco Polo
looked into a valley, and with clouds between,
saw horsemen swarm like beetles and running ant-men
overtaken. They were too far to fall:
he guessed their deaths when one of every two
stopped in his tracks. "There never was a war
so lost in space," he said. "I heard the wind,
and the long scratch of an eagle's cry adrift,
and I saw the running and stopping between clouds."

It was his first and last sight of that place.
He moved East, a thousand leagues yet,
to splendors and strange customs. And returned,
and could not find again in the mountain mazes
that valley below the clouds. "There was a village,"
he said in his wine, "and after the running and stopping,
the beetles entered with torches and, fire-flushed,
another scribble of ants ran and was stopped.
Then the smoke made a squall in the valley's throat:
black cloud under white clouds, and the sun dropping.
My horses and men were waiting. We were few
and had far to go. *Tibon* they call that country,
and the souls of men need God's sinews to cross it.
We saw the backs of eagles but never their breasts.
And descended at last, losing our best by the way:
burials at piled stones in the wind that snatched prayer
unspoken from our mouths, screams like fissures in the air
plunging away from the ledges. We came to the Emperor—
afire in silks and carbuncles, he sat rat-faced in splendor,
an uncombed hemp of whiskers strung from his chin.
—And returned. Honored. With gifts. Returned,
tugging our souls once more over God's backbone.
Losing our gifts and companions. Arriving with no more

than seeds, the dish of the little strings, and the powder that burns
with many colors and a great sound."

He was slow in the telling.
His voice said more than his words of the time it is
over the ridge of the world. And what are splendors
in their rat-faces? Of all the brinks he walked,
it was one valley my countryman Marco Polo
returned to most in the slow nights over wine.
An old man he was in my prime and I listened in reverence.
Great brow, great mane, he seemed a white lion thinking.
"It is myself I see from a cliff past cloud,
my struggles small and soundless, and my companions
shed from the last ledge under God. Whose dwarf I am.
Whose traveler I was once. Whose dusts I stir
remembering." Said my countryman Marco Polo,
these forty years away to the dusts I sit in.

That noon we banged like tubs in a blast from Hell's mouth.
Axes donged on casques, and the dead steamed through their armor,
their wounds frying. Horses screamed like cats, and men
ran through their own dust like darks howling. My country
went up in flames to the last rick and roof, and the smoke
was my own breath in me scorching the world bare.

We fought. May the clerk eat his own hand in fire forever
who wrote I would not face Arthur. Iron sparks iron.
We fought as we had been made, iron to iron. Who takes
a field from me tastes his own blood on it.
Three times I knocked him from the saddle. What's a king?—
he'd had the best mare ever danced on turf

and couldn't sit *that* saddle. Well, I rode her:
king's mount from bell to cockcrow while bed, castle, and country
shook under us, and he snored holiness to a sleeping sword
from the fairies. Excalibur's ex-horseman. Yes, I fought him:
I took my damnation as it came and would have hacked
a thousand Arthurs small to mount her again.

He did better by a warhorse. That saddle, at least, he knew
how to climb into. Iron to iron he charged, and could have knocked
a castle over. But still a fool, too pure for a feint
or sidestep. Three times I dumped him with his ribs stove
and could have finished him backhand, but reined and waited
with my own head split and a puddle of blood in my pants.

The fourth, he hove dead already into the saddle and came on.
But even a king won't work with no blood in him:
his point dropped till it grounded, and poled him
over his horse's rump. And I did not rein but took him
clean in air, though I broke my arm to do it. And there he lay:
my two horns on his head, my third through his back.

What can a clerk know of the day of dead kings and dead countries?
I blew and no one answered. The men were dead
and scarcely boys enough left to carry a king's bones
to the smoke of the burned chapel. What other burial
was done that day was done by crows and gypsies. And in my heart:
where would I find another worth damnation?

I never turned back and I never looked back. My country
burned behind me and a king lay skewered on a charred altar,
his sword in blood at my feet. I took it up and flung it
into a swamp. He had bled into it: why hold back his sword?
No fairy arm reached out of the muck to catch it. That
was another life and spent, and what was there left to save?

Except the mare! Even bled down to dust and my bones shivered,
my veins pumped at the thought of her. Why else
had I cracked king, castle, and my own head? I rode,
and mended as I rode—mended enough—enough to be still alive—
or half alive—when I found her. And when I had waited
a cool two hours at her door, what came to meet me?

A nun! Eight thousand men dead and the best iron in England
black in the burned stones of a burned shire, and my own bones
stitched in by nothing but scars, and there she stood,
black as the day we had made of the world, and gave me
—a litany of tears! A whore of heaven wailing
from a black cassock as if she stood naked in a hollow tree!

With her eyes turned in unseeing: as if to Heaven:
as if there were no world and we had not dared it
beyond damnation! That was the death of all:
she dared not even look at what we were! And for *this*
I had fed the best meat in England to carrion crows
and left a crown in mud for a gypsy's picking.

I did not turn back and I did not look back.
I had left a king and country dead without turning.
Should I turn now for a mare? Let Heaven ride her spavined:
I had the heat of her once, and I'd sooner
have turned Saracen and ripped the crosses from Europe
than deny my blood spilled into his in the field that made us.

Once of a world she danced like flame, and the man who would not
die to be scorched there was dead already. Dead as the clerk
who rhymed us to a moral. There is no moral. I was. He was. She was.
Blood is a war. I broke my bones on his, iron to iron.
And would again. Without her. Stroke for stroke. For his own sake.
Because no other iron dared me whole.

Mortmain, the Devil's hook, black-flaking,
Reached out for Byron, not for final taking
But in an introductory way, for shaking.

"How do you do?" and "Pray be not alarmed."
—That sort of thing. —"What poet was ever harmed
By coming on a theme?" His smile disarmed
All second thought. And Byron: "Sir, I'm charmed."

Well, so he had his theme. Book after book
He piled up every prop that rhymed with hook.
Nothing he rhymed was quite the hook he took

There on that hilltop of the dead of night.
"Byron," he signed. A silly oversight:
The Devil had said, "George Gordon, Sir? Of Gight?"

Maybe at Missolonghi, as the air
Fogged out its last, its tremor sketched a pair
Of fine dark fellows, very debonair,
Who met at night and shook hands for a dare,
At which one cried, "There, Mother! Damn you! There!"

51 ► Damn Her

Of all her appalling virtues, none
leaves more crumbs in my bed, nor
more gravel in my tub
than the hunch of her patience
    at its mouseholes.

She would, I swear, outwait
the Sphinx in its homemade quandaries
once any scratching in the walls
has given her to suspect
    an emergence.

It's all in the mind, we say. With her
it's all in the crouch, the waiting
and the doing indistinguishable. Once
she hunches to execution, time is merely
    the handle of the switch:

she grasps it and stands by for whatever
will come, certainly, to her sizzling
justice. Then, inevitably always daintily
she closes her total gesture
    swiftly disdainfully as

a glutton tosses off a third dozen
oysters—making light of them—as if
his gluttony were a joke that all
may share. (The flaps and bellies
    of his grossness

are waiting, after all, for something
much more substantial than
appetizers.) —"Bring on the lamb!" her look
says over my empty shells. "Bring on
    the body and the blood!"

I said to her tears: "I am fallible and hungry,
and refusal is no correction and anger no meal.
Feed me mercies from the first-bread of your heart.

I have invented no part of the error it is
to be human. The least law could jail me
and be upheld; the least theology, damn me

and be proved. But when, ever, have I come to you
to be judged? Set me straight to your last breath,
and mine, and feed me most what I need not deserve

—or starve yourself, and starve me, and be right."

You think it was easy—those years at point-of-fox?
smelling the enemy's guess before he guessed it?
moving one hand in light and one in dark?
living forever in two minds at once?
It was not easy: it was a way of life.

I listened: fox a-twitch for the blood stir.
Wars are won in the listening. Women sell secrets.
Men—the good ones—sob them on the rack.
I lay in one foul bed, stood by the other.
And listened. I moved in my own stench—but I won.

My days binged off. I woke lean to a bellyful
of cannonbread. Ten thousand gutted horses
screamed as they spilled: the burst heart-springs,
the strained haunches buckling, the carcasses
trembling to dead tapers from the rump's hummock.

I remember the horses and not the men.
The agony in the avalanche trailed back
no cry but the long scree of the animal.
The terror in lashed water, the surge and crumple
under the firefalls, the crazed alert too late

at the boiling centers when the bolt-swarms chirred
and the sky went dark as under a wheel of starlings—
only the flung hammerhead slobbering, and the eye of the beast
like the ball of fat forced out of a lance wound
comes back from all those dying victories.

I saw at last: men were at war with horses:
the dead died by accident in their passion
to ride the beast's blood out between their knees:
there was no battle and no victory
but the field strewn with the beast's innocence.

. . . I threw the world away but I could not lose it:
my kingdom ruled me: I sent criers to peace:
night nickered back: ten thousand thousand horses
leaped like a fire and blew their deaths out on me.
I won again before I knew I fought:

my storms, already coiled, broke of themselves
to pile the dead before me. So I learned:
what is victory but a way of life?
I am king of death. I watch my crown and listen.
There is no end to what a king begins.

I said to the pear-shaped darling
where she sat like a bulge in the light:
"Love is no thought, I think. We open and close
like the locks of your moods upon you.
Love, you say, *Say you love me.*
What are you thinking that you will not say it?
—But were we to think once, even your
body would be shapeless. And were we to think enough,
what reason could keep us from mercy?

Once after sex I was all bray inside
and aching as if from a marathon. Now,
it is a little sad to give so little.
Even the eyes of monks could seem reasoned.

Then sadness itself becomes a thought.
Then an intellect beyond reason hungers
for the peace of your spent body.
Then, like no thought, there happens
a pity almost love that turns to love.

Save me from too much memory in the act.
We are desperate together and born to praise.
I will cry love—in some vocabulary—
till mercy be the name our sleeps abound,
and grace beget us easy presences."

—*News Item*

It is time to break a house.
What shall I say to you
but torn tin and the shriek
of nails pulled orange
from the ridge pole? Rip it
and throw it away. Beam
by beam. Sill, step, and lintel.
Crack it and knock it down.
Brick by brick. (I breathe
the dust of openings. My tongue
is thick with plaster. What can I
say to you? The sky has come
through our rafters. Our windows
are flung wide and the wind's
here. There are no doors
in or out.) Tug it
and let it crash. Haul it.
Bulldoze it over. What can I say
to you except that nothing
must be left of the nothing
I cannot say to you. It's
done with. Let it come down.

Ten thousand vegetarians in Istanbul
demonstrated against a shipment of blood puddings
from Overseas Relief, and that started it.

Before Parliament had finished asking questions
Congress was on the street with answers,
and before the edition was sold out, the OSS
had proved to the CIC that the puddings
had been made from diverted plasma. The plasma,
moreover, though ostensibly donated
by the undergraduate body of the University
of Northwest El Paso (and clearly so stenciled),
had in fact been made by pulping wetbacks
in an illegal wine factory. Residual
impurities established that. Worse yet,
the shipment in question was a fourth squeezing.
—And in a very poor vintage year, mind you.

The President, informed by Aerial Survey Teams
that there was no University of Northwest
El Paso, had one organized overnight.
Crash priority. They stocked it, for a start,
with a brigade of marines and two companies
of WAC's. The faculty, of course, was FBI.

That got around the worst of the embarrassment
(though the Mexican ambassador remained
persistent about claims for wine taxes
and had finally to be bought off). It could be made
to look like an honest mistake. It was even
arranged to have the U of NWEP Whirlwinds
win the Rose Bowl Game that year. Nothing
was too much trouble, you may be sure,
when the National Security was at stake.

But there was still the problem of getting those
ten thousand vegetarian agitators in Istanbul
to shut up and eat their blood puddings
like grateful little carnivores. That took some doing.

The OSS tried dehydrating it all over again
then mixing it with surplus Coca Cola.
They should have known how sensitive those Turks
are about anyone else's imperialism,
but who can tell the State Department anything?
Worse, the Bulgarians got their hands on a case of it
and were able to prove that venous injections
of the stuff killed sheep. That's when the Russians
started to holler "Bacteriological Warfare."
And there we were embarrassed all over again.

So we took the Coca Cola out of it
(which was some process, believe me)
and we started slipping the stuff into
shipments of cherry pie. You might have guessed
that wouldn't work. Actually, the White House
was against the idea from the start
but the Amalgamated Bakeries Lobby had this overstock
and managed to stampede Congress.

And there we were embarrassed all over again
with ten thousand vegetarian Turkish agitators
still howling, and this time barricaded
behind eight million cherry pies. They even
planted mines in some of them, as a result of which
we lost two tanks, and eighteen farm boys
from Iowa, Missouri, Illinois, and Kansas,
who just couldn't resist snitching a pie or two.
Our boys always did have that weakness
for cherry pie. Reminds them of Mom, I guess.

Well, by now American blood had been spilled
and anybody that can remember the Maine,
the Alamo, or Primo Carnera mauling Jack Sharkey,
knows what that means. Nobody
is going to embarrass us and make us like it.
Least of all ten thousand vegetarian agitators,
and Turks to begin with.

                           That's when we dropped
ten thousand commandos specially trained
in changing parachutes into Arab costumes.
Nobody knows yet what happened to the
vegetarian Turks, but all at once Istanbul
was full of Arabs screaming for blood pudding,
and in no time at all we had ourselves
a propaganda triumph. Best of all
the Arabs decided to stay, so we let them take over
Turkey. After that, Israel was a cinch,

and Syria, and Jordan. And when Egypt begged us,
in a slightly Brooklyn accent, to take over the Suez—
well, you just gotta give the President credit.
It was his idea in the first place. And what I say is,
if you really want your freedom from them vegetarians,
it takes a military man to handle the hot ones.

Leaving—for the present—sunsets, bluebirds, pussywillows,
and all that is not in itself saccharined,
sentimentalized, or otherwise disgusting, but which
has been marzipan'd, or, to phrase from the French, enmerded,
by the fact that there are females in our culture,
and certain attitudes evolving those females
into a species of converging vacuities
(as befits, in time, the mothers of storm troopers,
sleepwalkers, enuretics, and total abstainers),
and considering nature not as décor but as energy—
a dynamics best observed in the corruption
of all organic compounds, each of which,
in process, tends to magnetize to itself
gnats, midges, maggots, rats, piranhe, buzzards,
molds, flies, beetles, hyenas, lobsters, gulls,
and all that locus of forces implicit
in the unwinding of the nebulae and the blast
of the gassy galaxies cooling into life,
of which the sunset is a modulation, and bluebirds
and pussywillows two variations
in the key of mothermilk and the clutching gut;
and any one of which stands ready to convert
my eyes, the adenoids of the dean of women,
or the soft tissue of Lydia Pinkham's
cerebellum, genitalia, viscera, et cetera,
into the soft tissue of everything else
(and the shell around it), wherever and whenever
anything waits with a food-sac to be filled—

I can think of no valid reason whatever
for not ignoring the most part of all ladies
(and gentlemen) at the weekly, bimonthly, or annual
meeting of practically everything with teacups,

or against the utter damnation of all Good Women,

and I will recommend accordingly
the debauchment of daughters, the extinction of maiden aunts,
sterilization of clergy, reallocation of zippers,
an embargo on tombstones, the impeachment of Congress,
the immediate promotion of all bartenders
to the status of customer, and, for a beginning—
with a pause for a black damnation on all opposed—
the bottle on the bar and a round on the house.

I should have something to say of/to this
woman who has had so little to say to
me, but who has said something, certainly,
to someone; while trying, with all the intensity
of the emancipated female, to speak to
all. Something. I do not like her, but she is
a poet, if only as The Free Woman. Something.
Well, then, what?

　　　　　　Emancipated, the slave
kept his chains for sentiment and making, now,
the motions of the free man, set them to clanking
so hard at every sweeping gesture, that his
free words were drowned in the sentiments
he brought to his freedom.

　　　　　　That is one
thing I might say of/to her. And of freedom,
that the line between eternal vigilance and some
clinically noted anxiety states is a jittery
one.
　　　Well, have it out. What else?

By a certain age, virginity is no longer
a preserved possibility but a lost chance.
Whatever had been an act of will in such
purity, changes into an enforced condition.
There comes to mind, also, a friend of mine
who saved a bottle of Calvados for a
sufficient occasion. He had brought it from France
in 1919, and had not found an occasion sufficiently
sufficient until 1945, when he opened it to celebrate
V-J Day; only to find that it had spoiled,
though the bottle remained as authentic
as one could wish.

I could say that to this
woman/poet. And of apple juice,
that it will not necessarily keep till another
war is over.

But I am only speaking distrusts.
She is, after all, a poet of some accomplishment.
And if one cannot trust poets toward humanity,
we shall all be at the mercy of preachers,
politicians, and related et ceteras.

What, then, shall
I say toward meaning, of this woman I do not like
who is an accomplished poet I do not admire,
because, as I see it, no amount of accomplishment
undoes silliness?

How do you do, Miss B?
Isn't it a lovely day for painting bearded irises
on the walls of the girls' locker room?

—And so I have either found nothing to say
in honor of my own profession, which is in praise
of the power of the enlarging word; or there is nothing
to say except what must be said of us all:
that there are no pure human states, and that any
pretension to one is an assertion of inhumanity.

Between my right big toe, sir, and my bent
first podlet, is a blister with my
very self's rubbed acutest small
part inside, swollen. —And why
tell you? —Because I
am too easily nothing to invent
sweats and itches for the ball
of any foot. As flesh is true,
every one of my toes is all about you.

I say "I" in the big name of
everyone's most likeness to
whatever is nearest the one who
rambles to sleep down crooked nerves,
but strait and straight dreams love.
I dream what whispers as it curves
kissing fingertips, skin by skin,
to the very I of what's locked in.

Every "I" I think to name
is a first person and singular
as any self that rose and came
out of its skin and fistula
since skin began to take its lumps;
from the missing link to the missing name
of the dream from which the monkey jumps.
And "Better to itch than not, God knows,"
whispers a truth between my toes.

And where is there any itch to feel
but singular, personal, and first?
"I" is the only I that's real
and "I" the only thirst:
everyone's "I" to the smallest cleft

hidden away in the tiniest peel
of the only skin we all have left.
"I" from dandruff to flaking toes
is everyman and how he goes.

Where is there any "They" within?
And where a skin too thick to itch?
Every dog is a son of a bitch,
sniffing the unders of all there is
and flea'd fast to his own dog skin.
"They" come dressed. But where is
any dog with any flea
but scratches naked as you and me?
Every dog is the dog there is.

Creeping near or running far,
every dog is the dog there is,
first person and singular.
And I am just the dog you are.

III ▸ NATURES

Once on Saipan at the end of the rains
I came on a flooded tire rut in a field
and found it boiling with a galaxy
of pollywogs, each millionth micro-dot
avid and home in an original swarm.

For twenty yards between the sodden tents
and a coral cliff, a universe ran on
in a forgotten dent of someone's passing.
Clusters and nebulae of whirligigs
whorled and maddened, a burst gas of life

from the night hop of unholdable energy.
Did one frog squatting heavy at the full
of its dark let out this light, these black rapids
inside the heart of light in the light-struck dent
of the accidental and awakened waters?

There on the island of our burning, in man's place
in the fire-swarm of war, and in a sunburst
lens, I stood asking—what? Nothing.
Universes happen. Happen and are come upon.
I stood in the happening of an imagination.

Ten days later, having crossed two seas,
I passed that rut again. The sun had burned
the waters back to order. The rut lay baked.
Twenty upthrust shoreline yards of time
slept in the noon of a finished imagination.

And the bed and the raised faces of the world
lay stippled with the dry seals of the dead,
black wafers with black ribbons, as if affixed
to a last writ, but with such waste of law,
I could not read its reasons for its proofs.

for Fletcher and Inga

Benny, the albino marmoset,
eighteen years old, balding, and arthritic,
crawls upside down in his cage by the geraniums,
his skin flaps heaving cords
and knots of labor.
                Eighteen for a marmoset
is older than nature, longer than Law allows
acrobats to stiffen and heave
on perches hunted by such talons
as even the quick must answer to.
                       Benny
puzzles a man-face out against the mesh,
two million years away from the cocktail party
we left the tree to come to.
Two by two
           we pause and look at Benny.
His life outside the Law
makes eyes from nature to décolletage.
A mistress mercy tends him as we watch,
curling him in her palm.
                  He,
coils and languishes, and then, put back,
grinds out his acrobatics for a grape,
from this world into that, one mesh
further from or nearer
                 some reality
martinis imagine in us or forget,
some day as it is with objects side by side,
looked at unequally by those pink eyes,
and ours, and thus, in fact, unequal.

Once in Canandaigua, hitchhiking from Ann Arbor
to Boston in the middle of December, and just
as dark came full on a stone-cracking
drill of wind that shot a grit of snow,
I was picked up outside an all-night diner
by a voice in a Buick. "Jump in," it said. "It's cold."

Four, five miles out, in the dead winter of nowhere
and black as the insides of a pig, we stopped.
"I turn off here."
       I looked around at nothing.
"The drive's up there," he said.
          But when I was out,
he headed on, turned round, drove back, and stopped.

"You haven't thanked me for the ride," he said.

"Thanks," I said, shuffling to find a rock
I might kick loose and grab for just in case.
But he wasn't that kind of crazy. He just waved:
"You're welcome, brother. Keep the rest for change."
Then he pulled in his head and drove away —
back toward Canandaigua.
        I thought about him
a good deal, you might say, out there in the sandblast
till a truck lit like a liner picked me up
one blue-black inch from frostbite.
And off and on for something like twenty years
I've found him in my mind, whoever he was,
whoever he is—I never saw his face,
only its shadow—but for twenty years
I've been finding faces that might do for his.
The Army was especially full of possibles,
but not to the point of monopoly. Any party

can spring one through a doorway. "How do you do?"
you say and the face opens and there you are
back in the winter blast.

But why tell you?
It's anybody's world for the living in it:
You know as much about that face as I do.

Even wisteria, sufficiently looked at,
will do for a galaxy. Nebulae
coil and flare on the trellises
of invisible principle much as these
gnarls and bursts grow to a house
they obliterate. With care then,
with waiting for a leaf to turn,
you may see the lives take place
in the great gaps of the system.
As at the porch corner there,
that nest full of raging fluffs,
half bald yet, who work mouths
the size of their entire heads
up into space. A nest of birds
is a nest of flames leaping,
novas of the insatiable energy.
Only the mercies of size save us—
imagine fledglings the size of rhinos
and full of just such rages—
what would a man do then
for the courage to look thoughtfully
into the throat of principle there
behind any leaf his waiting turns?

Watching a kettle boil, a puddle
burst into pollywogs, light
catch in an ice-edge and ray open,
one thinks—nothing to say. There are

rays in things and they open to silences.
All wet is a mother whose seeds
rage up to leave her. There is fire
under wet, and a first sound there

of forces forming through seas.
As time hissed once, uncontainably,
from the shell cooling. "Go down, Weather,"
said the Principal Midnight then,

"and set light, seed, and fire adrift.
Let there be demonstrations of courage.
I am tired of propounding theory
to my angels. Let them see practiced

how life will dare itself from any wet."

A man can survive anything except not caring
and even that's not mortal enough
to stop his drinking, except of course
that even drinking can be a kind of
                                    caring.

Sometimes it takes a kind of at least
heroism to look entirely at Eighth Avenue
without anesthetic. Where would a man
get the sort of courage that risks
                                    pity?

Frontiersmen maybe. Those whiskery hermits
that had to prove themselves to every
bear and redskin. But those were haters.
Which of them had the courage to risk a
                                    tear?

Not anyhow Joshua, the old rumpot. He's
not daring anything sober, least of all
the question. Assuming there's one left
in him. What question? You crazy? This is
                                    Joshua

you're talking about. "Hey, Mac," he says,
"buy a ticket to my funeral. Ringside
for one drink. Or sell you my left leg
for a pint. Going out of business. Everything must be
                                    sold.

Whattayasay? Everybody needs a funeral
to go to." —And so for the third time
this year I buy his left leg. And once more own
more pieces than I can put to one
                                    man.

In the hobble of imagination
the geranium there on the sill
clenches the muddy last
of its turkey-wattle bloom.

I taste an earth-name
for the dead going of colors.
But my schooling cheats the fact,
goes hooking for principle:

"Thing linked in thing," it buzzes
from the catholic shadow
where I was bent young
from nature to ordinance,

"meaning is first, then act,
then once more meaning.
Dying is of the chain. The tree
is born of its own leaves."

But the rotten green mud
in an overwatered stalk,
and the bloom, already humus
though still hanging, darken

from sun, sill, and imagination.
Not principle but its aberration—
a leak from green to black,
an escape without walls—

stains through sick changes
from sun to the unimaginable
last of love, and melts to dirty butter
the heart-stone of the lifted house.

They admired you
and I was proud.
They are good men
who are made happy
by happiness.

Dragons are not the only beasts
God forgot to make, and which, therefore,
man had, himself, to invent. The Phoenix,
the Griffin, the Sphinx, the Unicorn,
and such nightworks as the Vampire
and the Werewolf, are all
in the nature of the Imagined Kingdom.
And what good, in the long run, is Dominion
unless it is given over all
necessary beasts, real and imagined?

Therefore the Dragon, which—if it is true
that man must imagine at least one shape
moving alive for every dream in him—
images that dark in the jungle of dendrites
one man must run from and another attack,
to which every daughter must be thrown once,
and out of which any man may think to marry
a princess.

       Dragons, moreover,
being fire-breathers, do not catch cold—
and certainly all men need to imagine
not-sniffling.

       All these are realities, but
if you actually see a Dragon, check carefully
which reality you have been living in.

           To do so
may be very much to your advantage.

79 ▶ Beagles

for Kenneth Rexroth

Beagles have big eyes and wet noses
and when they fall in love with any
part of humanity they stay there
as if it were important.

Had beagles as much sense as incest
in their pedigrees, they might learn maybe
to squint a little, and to wipe their noses,
when they look at what they take for God.

A bird with a name it does not itself
recognize, and I cannot recall—
if ever I knew it, and no matter—
lives off the great gross Rhinoceros of Africa.

The slathering hide of the great gross Rhinoceros,
slabbed like a river in a stiff wind,
is rancid at the bent seams, and clogged
with lice and fly-grubs at the pores and pittings.

The Rhino-bird, whatever its unknown name,
attends its warty barge through the jungle,
the feast of its own need picking the tickle
of many small corruptions from behemoth,

who, impervious to all roarers, is yet defenseless, alone,
against the whine of the fly in his ear, and stricken
to helpless furies by the squirm of the uncoiling grub
tucked into the soft creases of the impenetrable.

My bird—and oh it is my bird and yours!—crawls
him as kissingly as saints their god, springs
circling over him to foretell all coming,
descends in the calm lapses to ride a-perch on his horn

or snout. Even into the mouth and nares of the beast
he goes—so some have reported—to pick infection
from power. And can the beast not love
the bird that comes to him with songs and mercies?

—Oh jungle, jungle, in whose ferns life dreamed itself
and woke, saw itself and was, looked back
and found in every bird and beast its feature,
told of itself, whatever name is given.

One day when I was feeling absolutely healthy
I climbed a mountain, and there at the top was
(just as I had absolutely foreknown—and what else
are mountains for to the absolutely healthy?)
the woman all mountains were standing for my health
to climb to.

Very few residents of Bronxville and/or their colleagues
transiently voting from a suburban address in
Connecticut, Jersey, or Long Island will know at once
the necessity of mountains to absolute health, or why
there is always that absolute woman there to be
climbed to.

As an absolute guess, I should say, at least one out of
every three thousand Tibetans might have an inkling of which
    mountain
such days as I mean come to. But perhaps I respect Tibetans
more for their distance from everyone I know than for
whatever they absolutely are inside themselves on their
best days.

Of you, my near brothers to nowhere on our level days
untopped, and of the imperfections of my own health
again and again in the days between topmost, and of the not-
    mountains
(like rotten nuts) that one forces only to find empty,
and of the anthills one falls from dusty into the splints
of sobriety,

and of the abysses between the ice cubes at 4:00 P.M. of a
Madison Avenue, and of all the partial women in cars
who wait in line for the 5:37 from Universe, and of all of us
plunging from the smoke-sided day at its stations, I make up
absolute Tibetans in an upper air of their best days
to dream us whole.

There was a squint-eyed holy man who shoved
a stone boat out to sea, to grind on ice
and preach to penguins how mankind was loved.
There he stood counting souls to Paradise.

So was I holy once till I went damned
flush in the best hour of my hocus-pocus.
Just as I dreamed of Heaven's Rose Bowl crammed,
my watery parishes swam into focus.

Our Father Birdsong, to these waddling flocks
which neither sing nor fly, and pass as men
to squinty saints, I pray send down Thy fox
to hunt Thy floes till they be clean again;

and till no man, for mercy, be misled
to dream of souls but that they sing and lift.
Till Thy saint die of joy and, rancid red,
Thy fox burn over him on the last drift.

An oyster that went to bed x-million years ago,
tucked itself into a sand-bottom, yawned (so to speak),
and woke a mile high in the Grand Canyon of the Colorado.

If I am not here for breakfast, geologize at will.